Animal Homes

Prairie Dogs and Their Burrows

by Martha E. H. Rustad

Consulting Editor: Gail Saunders-Smith, PhD

Consultant: William John Ripple, Professor
Oregon State University
Corvallis, Oregon

Mankato, Minnesota

Pebble Plus is published by Capstone Press
151 Good Counsel Drive, P.O. Box 669, Mankato, Minnesota 56002
www.capstonepress.com

1 2 3 4 5 6 09 08 07 06 05 04

Library of Congress Cataloging-in-Publication Data
Rustad, Martha E. H. (Martha Elizabeth Hillman), 1975–
   Prairie dogs and their burrows / by Martha E. H. Rustad.
   p. cm.—(Pebble plus: Animal homes)
   Includes bibliographical references (p. 23) and index.
   ISBN 0-7368-2584-3 (hardcover)
   1. Prairie dogs—Habitations—Juvenile literature. [1. Prairie dogs—Habitations.]
I. Title. II. Animal homes (Mankato, Minn.)
QL737.R68 R84 2005
599.36'7—dc22   2003024904

Summary: Simple text and photographs illustrate prairie dogs and their burrows.

Editorial Credits
Mari C. Schuh, editor; Linda Clavel, series designer; Enoch Peterson, book designer; Kelly Garvin,
   photo researcher; Karen Hieb, product planning editor

Photo Credits
Bruce Coleman Inc./Lee Rentz, 18–19
Corbis/W. Perry Conway, 15, 16–17
GeoImagery/James Roetzel, 13
James P. Rowan, 8–9, 21
Minden Pictures/Jim Brandenburg, cover, 6–7
Photodisc Inc./PhotoLink, 1
Tom & Pat Leeson, 5, 11

Note to Parents and Teachers

The Animal Homes series supports national science standards related to life science.
This book describes and illustrates prairie dogs and their burrows. The images support
early readers in understanding the text. The repetition of words and phrases helps early
readers learn new words. This book also introduces early readers to subject-specific
vocabulary words, which are defined in the Glossary. Early readers may need assistance
to read some words and to use the Table of Contents, Glossary, Read More, Internet Sites,
and Index/Word List sections of the book.

Word Count: 130
Early-Intervention Level: 15

Table of Contents

Burrows

Prairie dogs are
rodents. Prairie dogs
live in burrows.

Prairie dogs dig burrows
with their claws. Burrows
have mounds of dirt
around their openings.

Prairie dogs dig tunnels
and rooms in their burrows.
They line the rooms with
fur and plants.

Prairie dogs dig for days
to make their burrows.
They live in their burrows
for many years.

Prairie dogs leave their burrows to find food. They eat grass and other plants.

Prairie Dog Families

About 10 prairie dogs live together in a family group.

Female prairie dogs have two
to eight young prairie dogs.
The young prairie dogs stay
warm and safe in burrows.

Staying Safe

Prairie dogs bark to warn each other of danger. Then they hide in their burrows.

Prairie dogs stay safe in burrows. Burrows are good homes for prairie dogs.

Glossary

bark—to make a short, loud noise; prairie dogs get their name from their bark, which sounds like a dog's bark.

burrow—a tunnel or a hole in the ground; a prairie dog town is a large group of prairie dog burrows in the same area.

claw—a hard curved nail on an animal's foot; prairie dogs use their claws to dig burrows.

danger—a situation that is not safe

mound—a small hill; mounds of dirt surround the openings of prairie dog burrows; prairie dogs stand on the mounds to look for danger.

rodent—a mammal with large, sharp front teeth; prairie dogs, rats, and beavers are rodents.

Read More

Murphy, Patricia J. *Prairie Dogs.* Grassland Animals. Mankato, Minn.: Capstone Press, 2004.

Spilsbury, Louise, and Richard Spilsbury. *A Colony of Prairie Dogs.* Animal Groups. Chicago: Heinemann Library, 2004.

Woodward, John. *Prairie Dogs.* The Secret World Of. Chicago: Raintree, 2004.

Internet Sites

FactHound offers a safe, fun way to find Internet sites related to this book. All of the sites on FactHound have been researched by our staff.

Here's how:

1. Visit *www.facthound.com*

2. Type in this special code **0736825843** for age-appropriate sites. Or enter a search word related to this book for a more general search.

3. Click on the **Fetch It** button.

FactHound will fetch the best sites for you!

Index/Word List